Wild Animal Kingdom

EAGLES

GAIL TERP

BLACK
RABBIT
BOOKS

Bolt is published by Black Rabbit Books
P.O. Box 3263, Mankato, Minnesota, 56002.
www.blackrabbitbooks.com
Copyright © 2018 Black Rabbit Books

Jennifer Besel, editor; Grant Gould, interior
designer; Michael Sellner, cover designer;
Omay Ayres, photo researcher

Library of Congress Cataloging-in-Publication Data
Names: Terp, Gail, 1951- author.
Title: Eagles / by Gail Terp.
Description: Mankato, Minnesota : Black Rabbit Books, [2018] | Series:
Bolt. Wild animal kingdom | Audience: Age 9-12. | Audience: Grade 4 to 6.
| Includes bibliographical references and index.
Identifiers: LCCN 2016049996 (print) | LCCN 2017005246 (ebook) | ISBN
9781680721898 (library binding) | ISBN 9781680722536 (e-book) | ISBN
9781680724868 (paperback)
Subjects: LCSH: Eagles–Juvenile literature.
Classification: LCC QL696.F32 T47 2018 (print) | LCC QL696.F32 (ebook)
| DDC 598.9/42–dc23
LC record available at https://lccn.loc.gov/2016049996

Printed in the United States at CG Book Printers,
North Mankato, Minnesota, 56003. 3/17

Image Credits

Alamy: Accent Alaska, 26;
D125SWM, 18; Roger Tidman, 29 (left);
Dreamstime: Brian Kushner, 6; iStock: Kenneth
Canning, 4–5; National Geographic Creative: Domi-
nique Braud, 20–21; KLAUS NIGGE, 7 (right); Suzi Esz-
terhas/Minden Pictures, 19; Shutterstock: Alexander Raths,
25 (fish); A.S.Floro, 23 (bottom); ; Banet, 17 (top); Chepe
Nicoli, 11; Ed Ziegler, 29; Eric Isselee, 25 (egg, chipmunk);
FloridaStock, 25 (eagle); guentermanaus, 28 (right); Iakov
Filimonov, 25 (bear); Kletr, 3; Le Do, 25; Maciej J, 7 (middle),
14–15 (eagles); Marek Velechovsky, Back cover, 1; Monica Johan-
sen, 7 (left); objectsforall, 25 (top snake); Pablo Sebastian Rodri-
guez, 32; Patthana Nirangkul, 14–15 (background); Pichugin
Dmitry, 16; ragnisphoto, 12–13; Rich Carey, 23 (top); Rokopix,
Cover; sahir Ismail, 31; Sakdinon Kadchiangsaen, 25 (eaglet);
Sarah2, 25 (bottom snake); Steve Collender, 28–29; tea
maeklong, 8–9; Wildnerdpix, 17 (bottom)
Every effort has been made to contact copyright
holders for material reproduced in this book.
Any omissions will be rectified in subse-
quent printings if notice is given to
the publisher.

Contents

CHAPTER 1

A Day in the

An eagle **perches** at the top of a tree. Its sharp eyes watch the water below. Soon, the bird spots a fish. Spreading its huge wings, it swoops down. Its sharp **talons** are open and ready. At the water's surface, the eagle uses its talons to grab the fish. Then it flies back to the tree.

COMPARING
EAGLE
SIZES

Time to Eat

The eagle settles back in the tree. Holding the fish tight, it uses its powerful beak to eat. It pulls chunks of meat off the fish. Bite by bite, the eagle eats it all.

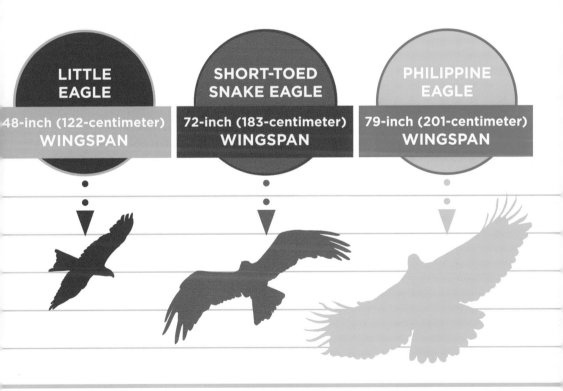

LITTLE EAGLE

48-inch (122-centimeter) **WINGSPAN**

SHORT-TOED SNAKE EAGLE

72-inch (183-centimeter) **WINGSPAN**

PHILIPPINE EAGLE

79-inch (201-centimeter) **WINGSPAN**

1.4 POUNDS
(0.63 kilogram)

4 POUNDS
(1.8 kilograms)

14 POUNDS
(6.5 kilograms)

EAGLE FEATURES

BEAK

EYE

TALONS

WING

FEATHERS

TAIL

CHAPTER 2

Food to Eat
and a Place to Live

About 60 types of eagles live in the world. Those types are often divided into four groups. Sea eagles live near water. Fish are the biggest part of their diet. Snake eagles are small. They mostly eat snakes. Booted eagles have feathers on their legs. They eat birds and **mammals**. Harpy eagles are very large. They eat mammals, such as monkeys and rabbits.

Home Sweet Home

Eagles live in many **habitats**.

Some live in forests close to shores.

Others live deep inside rain forests.

Some eagles live in deserts

or grasslands.

All eagles hunt for food. Some hunt from a perch on a tree. Others search for prey while flying. Most eagles hunt alone. But some hunt in pairs.

EAGLE RANGE MAP

Eagles live on every continent except Antarctica.

CHAPTER 3

Family Life

Male and female eagles pair up to **mate**. Eagle pairs often stay together for life. Most pairs build nests together. They use sticks and twigs. Then they line the nest with grass, leaves, or feathers. Eagles often use their nests year after year. The nests can get very large.

Where Do Eagles Build Their Nests?

CLIFFS

TREES

GROUND

Eaglets

Female eagles lay eggs once a year. They lay one to four eggs. But they don't lay them all on the same day. Females wait two to four days between laying each egg.

Males and females take turns sitting on the eggs. They sit on the eggs to keep them warm. Once the eggs hatch, the parents bring food to the eaglets.

Flight

In about two to three weeks, eaglets' feathers begin to grow in. When they're about 10 weeks old, eaglets try to fly. The young eagles' first flights might not go smoothly. But in time, they become strong fliers.

Many eagles can spot rabbits 2 miles (3 kilometers) away.

CHAPTER 4

Predators
and Other Threats

Humans have caused problems for eagles. Cutting down forests leaves fewer places for the birds to live. Chemicals used to kill insects are also trouble for eagles.

At least 10 types
of eagles are
endangered.

At Risk

Most adult eagles have no **predators**. But their eggs and eaglets are at risk. Birds, snakes, and lizards eat eagles' eggs and young. Even some bears will raid eagle nests.

This **food chain** shows what eats eagles.
It also shows what eagles eat.

SNAKES   BIRDS   BEARS

EGGS & EAGLETS

EAGLES

FISH

SNAKES

MAMMALS

25

Helping Eagles

People are now working to help eagles. Laws have set aside land where eagles can safely live. Other laws have stopped the use of harmful chemicals.

Eagles are amazing animals. They are some of the largest and most powerful birds in the world. People must work to protect these fierce fliers.

By the Numbers

5 INCHES
(13 cm)

10 to 30 years
LIFE SPAN OF WILD EAGLES

30 miles
(48 km) PER HOUR

A BALD EAGLE'S AVERAGE FLYING SPEED

2 EAGLE SPECIES IN NORTH AMERICA

1 HOLE IN A BALD EAGLE'S TONGUE THAT'S USED IN BREATHING

200 MILES (322 km) PER HOUR A GOLDEN EAGLE'S TOP DIVING SPEED

endangered (in-DAYN-jurd)—close to becoming extinct

food chain (FOOD CHAYN)—a series of plants and animals in which each uses the next in the series as a food source

habitat (HAB-uh-tat)—the place where a plant or animal grows or lives

mammal (MAH-muhl)—a warm-blooded animal that feeds milk to its young and usually has hair or fur

mate (MAYT)—to join together to produce young

perch (PURTCH)—to sit on or be on something high

predator (PRED-uh-tuhr)—an animal that eats other animals

prey (PRAY)—an animal hunted or killed for food

talon (TAH-luhn)—one of the sharp claws on the feet of some birds

BOOKS

Bodden, Valerie. *Eagle.* Grow with Me. Mankato, MN: Creative Education, 2015.

Gray, Susan H. *Harpy Eagle.* Exploring Our Rainforests. Ann Arbor, MI: Cherry Lake Publishing, 2015.

Jennings, Rosemary. *Eagles.* Raptors! New York: PowerKids Press, 2016.

WEBSITES

Bald Eagle
kids.nationalgeographic.com/animals/bald-eagle/#bald-eagle-closeup.jpg

Eagles and Their Types
www.reference4kids.com/birds/eagles_and_their_types.html

Golden Eagle
animals.sandiegozoo.org/animals/golden-eagle